C

The

Playground

Principle

10 Steps to Enhance

Your Working Partnerships

DAVID R. SMAT

ISBN: 0990413209

ISBN-13: 978-0990413202

ACKNOWLEDGMENTS

I want to thank my wife, Laurie, and sons Rob, James, Michael and Joey, and my editor Mary Venturella for their support of my writing endeavors. You are my true inspiration.

I also owe homage to my colleagues from the working playground, as the collective source of these personal lessons learned.

PREFACE

We are all busy ... much too busy to read a diatribe of doctoral dissertations or cognitive studies to teach us how to relate with difficult co-workers, manage our bosses, or lead cross-functional teams ... hence the purpose for this book.

Throughout every waking minute of our lives, whether at work, at the PTA meeting, or at home, we are faced with the uncontrollable element of personal relationships. These challenges morph daily, with an endless array of scenarios and personalities that boggle our minds and create great case studies for graduate theses and psychology texts. Just when we think we've figured it out, another unique situation presents itself.

This book is not a lengthy thesis or psychology text, and might take 15 minutes of your time to read. It will not cite study data that has been painstaking researched and summarized, nor will it quote well known professors or authors with myriad credentials and three letter certifications following their names. So, if you are looking for a more intense study of relationship psychoanalysis or the inner workings of the human brain segment that controls innate cognitive functions (assuming that this segment actually exists), then put this book back on the shelf in the local bookstore, or better yet, buy it and offer it as a white elephant gift during your next psychology study group party.

OK - now that we've confirmed that you are not in for a Psych 101 Lesson, here's the good news ... you already know most everything you need to become successful in your working partnerships. In fact, you've experienced many of these situations before, in varying scenarios, spanning the majority of your waking life.

The following ten short chapters will remind you of these distant learning events, and will help you rethink these crucial personal experiences, all of which can improve your current day working relationships.

Now that I've raised your curiosity, you may be asking yourself, "If I already know all of this, then what's the point in reading further?"

In response, I suggest that you keep an open mind and proceed to the next chapter, the beginning of which has much to do with your success in implementing the lessons presented in this book.

THE PLAYGROUND PRINCIPLE – AN INTRODUCTION

We all remember this day in our early childhood: We are 2 or 3 years old and it's time for our first lesson in relationship building, on a playing field fondly remembered as the "Playground."

We enter with no prior warning, no preparation or how-to books that define what we should do (such as this one). We are thrown head-first into the abyss of our first hands-on relationship building workshop, without having been afforded a pre-read or study guide.

Picture yourself standing there at the edge of the playground's wood chip boundary, keenly focused on the horsey tire swing with the braided rope tail or the lime green rocking alligator that is occupied by your future manager, co-worker or next door neighbor (all too early to be confirmed, but clearly possible in theory).

Inevitably, you wander over aimlessly to assume the seat of honor. This pre-empts lesson number one, as you are quickly dethroned and thrown to the ground by a behemoth with a red buzz-cut and what appears to be chocolate spread across his chubby cheeks. Through this simple personal experience you have learned that the direct approach may not always be the most effective, or the safest, so you retreat to your Mother for solace and a grape-flavored lollipop.

So it begins, with literal baby steps into the void of relationship building. Within a few days or weeks, you have rethought your approach and are riding the lime green rocking alligator with your new friends (or you resort to visiting the coveted alligator during off-hours, in hopes of a smaller, less aggressive group). Whether it was the offer of one of your grape lollipops or another tactfully used ploy to gain friendship, as a mere child you successfully created an effective working relationship.

Flash forward four more years as you enter the playground in kindergarten, with a very similar population, which may include the same feared redhead or his brother. The number and variety of children is greater this time, with equally varied personalities and cliques. Again, you must craftily work the maze of individuals to see where you best fit in, all the while avoiding the more volatile personalities, and a bloody nose.

These life forming experiences continue through middle school, into high school and college, and continue to the current day. Just as was witnessed on the playground, today you can look across the conference table at your co-workers or colleagues and see the red-haired behemoth, the kid with the runny nose, the football team captain, the cheerleader, the geek with the taped horn-rimmed glasses, the ever-present bully and, of course, the comedian. Other than being advanced in age and maturity (which is always a matter of opinion), we're working with the same personalities that we've grown up with during recess on the playground.

Back to the issue at hand: If much of what we have learned first-hand over the years forms the basis for current day encounters, why do we experience recurring problems in our working relationships? Have we forgotten our life-long lessons learned from the playground? Are we too busy or self-directed to be patient with our co-workers?

The answer is a solid, "Yes." We *are* too busy; we *do* tend to be self-directed and impatient with our colleagues and co-workers. This conveniently leads to the first of the ten Playground Principles, aptly called "Wind the Clock."

CHAPTER 1

BE PATIENT
(WIND THE CLOCK ... PAUSE, THINK, THEN REACT)

"He that can have patience, can have what he will."
(Benjamin Franklin)

"Patience and perseverance have a magical effect before which difficulties disappear and obstacles vanish."
(John Quincy Adams)

A friend of mine who is a C-130 Hercules pilot first introduced me to the idea of "winding the clock."

Specifically, whenever new pilots are in training, they are taught that when they are faced with an emergency situation, they should reach down and pretend to wind the clock on their instrument panel to calm their thoughts. During this pause, the pilots fully assess the conditions allowing them to most effectively take action. This idea dates back to the early T-37 trainer aircraft that had a spring loaded clock that required occasional winding by the pilot. The process is still used today, even in modern aircraft that have digital clocks that do not require winding. The simple premise behind "Wind the clock" is to pause, think the situation through, then reply ... In other words, be patient in your (re)action.

In relation to working partnerships, patience must come into play with each decision and response that you make. How many times have you left a discussion wishing you had not reacted so quickly, or wishing you had paused before overreacting? You will find that a well thought through response will trump the quick decision, every time. These few second delays are especially beneficial during heated conversations, preventing an outburst of emotions. It is perfectly acceptable to be silent for a few seconds, think through your response, and then reply. The initial silence may seem uncomfortable at first, but once you've collected your thoughts, the few second pause will be quickly forgotten.

So remember, pause and reflect for a second or two while you wind the clock, collect your thoughts, then respond--you can never take back a knee-jerk reaction. Don't crash the plane.

CHAPTER 2

RESPECT OTHERS

"I speak to everyone in the same way, whether they are the garbage man or the president of the university."
(Albert Einstein)

I cannot emphasize enough how a sincere display of respect for others will positively influence your working partnerships.

Unfortunately, many people are driven by the personal gain of who they converse with, who they are seen talking to, or who they are meeting for lunch. Of course there is a place and time for these one-on-one discussions, but do not neglect everyone in the room to catch a word with the authority of the moment. Realize that everyone has a role in the success of the organization, no matter how small a part they may play. Adopt this mindset, and re-engage the lessons learned dating back to your first step onto the playground, where your vision of each person was equal; else you ended up face-down in the wood chips.

But first, look deep into your memory for the leader that you most respect--whether that be a past baseball coach, your second grade teacher, or a current co-worker or senior executive. Is it a coincidence that they knew you by your first name, or that they had an uncanny ability to recall that you were newly married, just bought a new Vett or that you had two daughters in college? Absolutely not. These unique individuals pride themselves and have consciously trained their minds to respect you as their partner, to remember your name, to understand you as a person and recall the project or life demands that you are faced with. In their eyes, you are their equivalent, their friend. This is why they are who they are, and why others, such as yourself, are drawn to them for advice and solace.

You may be asking yourself, how do I become this person? I cannot remember names.

I am barely able to remember my own personal demands, much the less those of others.

The answer is simple. Just as on the playground where you initially did not know anyone, start from step one. That being a sincere openness towards all, without preconceived notions, judgment or other. Don't automatically look for friends in the crowd, instead enter with the intent to meet new acquaintances. Consider also, that each one of these new acquaintances has never heard of your current life stories, so you should never be at a loss for discussion material.

The next Chapter will aid you in gaining a respectful rapport with each new acquaintance you meet, contrary to the typical rules you have heard.

CHAPTER 3

BREAK THE GOLDEN RULE

"The Golden Rule is that there are no golden rules."
(George Bernard Shaw)

Everyone has been taught the Golden Rule: Treat others as you would like to be treated. This Rule is a misnomer.

Instead, break the Golden Rule by first getting to know your friends, colleagues or co-workers well enough to learn what makes them tick. Then treat them the way *they* would like to be treated, not the way you would desire.

Back to the playground. When you first entered this new world, would you have walked up to a new acquaintance and punched them in the arm to say hello, just as your friends might greet you? Absolutely not. You were cautious back then and approached each new acquaintance with open eyes and ears, looking for that connection to strike common ground.

So why has this changed in your current-day relationships? Why do we assume we know how others want to be treated, instead of Winding the Clock to observe and better assess their interests?

The answer is simple. Over the years since our playground days, our ability to pause and listen has lessened, reducing our effectiveness in truly engaging with our colleagues. We assume that we know best, thinking what we would want for ourselves is best for others.

How do we reverse this trend? As a suggestion, consider each person that you meet as an unknown, with new interests and needs. Don't assume, pre-judge or jump to conclusions. Then, be quiet, and listen openly to who they are. If this is uncomfortable, and you feel the need to recount your life story, force yourself to first ask them three questions about themselves. Listen intently, and let this introduction fuel your thoughts going forward. Give them the first chance, then follow with your intro.

So break the Golden Rule: Do onto others as they would do onto themselves, via an open mind, eyes and ears.

CHAPTER 4

AVOID THE RUMOR MILL

"Whoever gossips to you will gossip about you."
(Spanish Proverb)

"What some invent the rest enlarge."
(Jonathan Swift)

Let's return to the playground in Fifth Grade.

You've just learned from Sally that a new classmate named Sam just moved to your school from another local school, allegedly for starting a food fight. You also hear that it was a tremendous feat--Spaghetti sauce everywhere, forks in the ceilings, baloney slices on the walls, mashed potatoes in everyone's hair. Now Sam has been exiled to Fifth Grade at Eastman Lower School, ready and looking for the perfect opportunity to better his performance. Sam's new reputation and the accompanying message spreads like wildfire.

Sam quickly becomes an unquestioned legend to some students, and is avoided by others, especially at lunch time when all eyes are fixed on him. Is that apple or orange that he placed on his tray, a future projectile with the Principal's name on it? At PE class, when Sam throws the tennis ball from center field, it is clear to all that his arm is a cannon, specifically trained to propel an abundance of assorted fruit across the cafeteria.

Now you are Sam, wondering why the tough kids keep giving you high-fives, while other students just stare. You never received this attention at your previous school, where you were the star baseball pitcher; a school you begrudgingly had to leave when your family moved to Eastman.

All because of the rumor mill.

So goes the rule of rumor avoidance. It is human nature to want to know the inside story behind the crisis at hand. We inevitably feed on these exciting tidbits of juicy info, and relish at the fancy of being the communicator of this news. Knowledge is power, especially when you are the owner.

Beware. Don't be this guy or girl--do not succumb to the temptation. Think back to how many times you've been in Sam's situation, requiring a tedious unraveling of false tales to set things right. Remember this when you overhear the next rumor. Not to be pessimistic, but believe little of what you hear, and half of what you see. When your instincts say that something doesn't sound right, that is your subconscious telling you it is not so. Just walk away.

Avoid the rumor mill at all cost--else find yourself in Sam's shoes.

CHAPTER 5

BE YOURSELF

"Be yourself, everyone else is already taken."
(Oscar Wilde)

"Be yourself--not your idea of what you think somebody else's idea of yourself should be."
(Henry David Thoreau)

Building on Chapters 2 and 3, the emphasis on Respect and breaking the Golden Rule continues in this chapter.

Consider the message of this chapter as the "opposite" of the Golden Rule: Never change who you are to become popular, or to mirror what you think others want you to be.

On the playground, everyone wants to be popular, with some going to extremes to make this happen. This sometimes involves going outside our normal persona, to match the likes or dislikes of the popular group. The comment that "Everyone likes James," or that "Susan is liked by all," is the ultimate compliment.

You might ask yourself, is your current environment that much more complex than the playground? The answer is "yes." We have more complex stressors than in our younger years, and have lost the innate ability to draw from these distant lessons learned on the playground, and wind the clock.

In our rushed existence, when we meet people for the first time, we tend to judge them within the first 15 seconds. We assess how they look or dress and develop our approach, attempting to gain their acceptance by similarities in our personality, function, life experiences, etc. Our goal is to gain common ground, to establish a comfort in relationship, or to assume this is not possible, at which point we disengage and escape to another more approachable individual or group.

This process, if performed properly, can be a very effective means to develop a working relationship, via "Winding the Clock," open mindedness and respect. Successfully performed, we find ourselves riding the tire horsey swing, or joining the company golf team. On the other hand, improper use by portraying a false impression, then you find yourself sitting on the edge of the playground, without a means of re-entry.

As an example, how many of us have approached the athletic circle of girls on the high school playground, due to the draw of one girl's jacket portraying the school volleyball team's insignia. You quickly attempt your "in" via discussions of your sister who played volleyball and your love for sports in general. In actuality, you may be a bookworm, who goes to sporting events out of obligation. If you were to continue down this path without first asking questions of them, you would never learn that the volleyball jacket was a gift from Anna's sister who graduated last year and is now in her freshman year in college, and that you were talking with the school's debate team captain, who couldn't tell you rule one about volleyball.

And so it goes. We assume a role that we think others want us to be, blind to the reality that we may already have a connection, if we were to just deliver the truthful message of who we are.

So remember, reverse the Golden Rule of engagement, and be truthful in who you are. Whether with your boss, your coworkers or the father who sits next to you at the middle school field hockey game, it's easier to be you than someone else.   In the end, people will like you for who you are, not for who they think you are-- just ask James, the popular one in high school.

CHAPTER 6

FOCUS ON YOUR STRENGTHS, NOT YOUR WEAKNESSES

"Focus on your potential instead of your limitations."
(Alan Loy McGinnis)

One of the more common words of advice you will hear is to improve your weaknesses.

The desired end-state apparently is a fully well-rounded person, without any weaknesses. What a concept.

Here's the scoop--this is a ridiculous suggestion. Even though every bookstore boasts a bookshelf of textbooks on improving your weaknesses, force yourself to think otherwise. Do *not* solely concentrate on your weaknesses; instead, work on improving your strengths. You will be happier and experience more successes, in contrast to being miserable as you woefully try to deal with your personal incapability.

When you were in Third Grade, would it have made sense that you would try out for the school musical if you were not a good singer? When you were in Fifth grade, would you have competed in the school spelling bee if you were a haphazard speller? Absolutely not. Even as an adolescent, you would avoid either of these opportunities like the plague. So why would this same notion make sense now, as an adult? It doesn't.

In the workplace, it is amazing how many people volunteer for tasks that they think their partner, manager or colleague thinks they are best suited for. Even though reality stares them straight in their face, they offer, "Sure, I can do that presentation." In the end, it's a disaster, after days of preceding stress, pages of speaker notes, uncomfortable practice sessions and gnashing of teeth.

So when you are one day faced by Susie Manager, who asks for volunteers to join the

Toastmasters Club (assuming you despise public speaking), pleasantly say "no." Do what is right for you. Avoid the stress and resentment, just to make Susie happy.

Concerning your strengths, the difficulty lies in knowing what these really are. Go back to the bookstore where you purchased this book, and you will find a plethora of strengths assessment books. Ironically, these books are surprisingly effective in capturing your strengths, with results that may surprise you. Within a few hours, you will have a list of your top strengths. Concentrate on these, and life in general will be that much more enjoyable.

So capture your strengths; build on them and your happiness at the same time.

CHAPTER 7

BE A POSITIVE ROLE MODEL

"For myself, I am an optimist ... It does not seem to be much use being anything else."
(Winston Churchill)

"We awaken in others the same attitude of mind that we hold toward them."
(Elbert Hubbard)

We all have bad days when things don't turn out as expected or unforeseen events negatively impact our behaviors and attitude.

These events may lead us to become overly critical of ourselves and personally demotivated.

Such negative emotions can be read on our faces and in our actions, especially by those we frequently partner with and even those who do not know us as well. In these instances of our displayed duress, friends, co-workers, and acquaintances will assume the worst; personalize our bad karma, and may even assume they are the cause. They will often avoid you, and wonder what they have done. Be aware 24/7 how your outward actions influence others--and avoid the transferral of negativity at all cost.

One key trait of successful and engaging leaders is how they react to bad days, while positively impacting others' perception of same. People flock towards individuals who exude positivity, as they too want to be part of a winning team. We've all seen this on the playground. In contrast, people run from those with a negative attitude. Why? Simply because they are a downer.

Do you remember Donny from high school? Everything he discussed had a negative spin, whether it was the cafe food, the English teacher, or the amount of homework received over the weekend. Talking with Donny was a chore, and over the school year, Donny would gather with the other naysayers, on the far side of the playground.

Donny has since grown up (or at least he is older), and now works in the cubicle next to yours. Throughout the day, you can hear his comments that his chair is uncomfortable, it's too hot or cold outside, or his weekend was miserable. He is also the first in line to complain about or to another co-worker. He's still a downer, and you avoid him like the plague ... and you should. Don't be a Donny downer. Intentionally try to be positive, both inside and outside of the workplace.

Clearly, this is difficult to do, hence the need for self-awareness. Be aware of your facial expressions, such as when your eyes roll every time Karen offers ideas at the weekly Staff meeting. Realize also that your colleagues in the room may catch your eye roll, and may unconsciously adopt this visual opinion of Karen, without even knowing her. Your same eye roll may have prevented her from being picked for the basketball game, as the teams were chosen back on the playground.

Be self-aware--and be positive. Others are watching, and they will follow your positivity.

CHAPTER 8

MAKE YOURSELF AVAILABLE

"An open door invites callers."
(Turkish Proverb)

When we were in middle school, one of the most feared and effective punishments was a ban from recess.

Many of us can remember sitting on a bench at the edge of the playground or alone in the classroom or library, looking out through the window at your friends playing. This also may have been the day that your recess football team lost without you as the quarterback, running back or receiver. You feel personally responsible ... you have let your friends down.

In effect, you have let your friends down-- not necessarily by directly causing the loss, but by not being there to provide support.

Today, this environment could figuratively relate to a sports team, but more likely involves a project team or study group, where your lack of presence causes a negative impression on your colleagues. Don't be this guy or girl. You must at all cost be there to support your partners. You should adopt an open door policy, fostering a safe environment for any questions.

As you progress in your career, you will inevitably be overworked with a bare minimum of time for one-on-one discussions. You will easily get lost in your daily schedule, with double- and triple-booked meetings becoming the norm. Your e-mail responses will diminish. You will have no time--Zero.

This is when you must rise above the challenge, and assure one-on-one personal time with your colleagues, direct reports, etc. Do not underestimate how important these meetings are, to include reasonably quick response to e-mail. This commitment will help solidify your collective rapport, keep you well able to reverse the Golden Rule, and maintain a strong affinity between you and your friends or team. If you choose to not remain available the odds are stacked against you that you will lose the football game.

Don't let them down--be there to play and win the game.

CHAPTER 9

ENCOURAGE OTHERS

"Instruction does much, but encouragement everything."
(Johann Wolfgang Von Goethe)

At the far corner of the playground, a baseball game has started, with a whiffle ball and bat that Jimmy received for his birthday.

Your friend Judy is up to bat, and you are cheering her on from the sideline. You know that Judy is not the athletic type, but she felt drawn to play because the new cute guy, Randy, selected her from the crowd to join his team, to her great delight. The problem is that Judy couldn't hit a beach ball with a snow shovel, much the less a whiffle ball with a 2-inch diameter round plastic bat. Nevertheless, you cheer her on.

Judy hears your cheers, looks over to you, and winks, as the first pitch passes her by. "Watch the ball," you scream, followed by "You can do it"!

Much to everyone's surprise, especially Judy's, she blindly swings at the second pitch, makes contact, and the ball flies over the second baseman's head. "Run," you scream, and Judy is off and running--to 3rd base, where she is eventually tagged out.

Your encouragement to Judy after this personal embarrassment to go talk to Randy pays off, as you later see Judy and Randy laughing with each other, as they discuss the mishap. Encouragement goes a long way, and should never be underestimated.

Would Judy have hit the ball, without your encouragement? Maybe.

Would she have approached Randy, after the fact, without your encouragement? Probably not.

Our words of encouragement are very powerful, more so than we realize. We are able to influence others by our words, and actions, as we learned very early in life, from personal experience as the giver, as well as the receiver. Encouragement can provide the motivation driving us to win, or the solace when we do not. Either way, it enables us to stay in the game.

Throughout our lives, we can each recall times when encouragement made the difference, whether it provided perseverance at the spelling bee, or the confidence to return to the batter's box after getting hit by a pitch. We all remember the day when our father or mother removed the training wheels from our bicycle, and their words of encouragement after we fell to the ground a few minutes later.

Encouragement is priceless. Don't underestimate its power--use it at every opportunity.

CHAPTER 10

BUILD YOUR NETWORK

"You only win when you help others win."
(Paul Zane Pilzer)

Most accomplishments are a result of Teamwork, and seldom solely due to individual effort.

There are situations where this may not be the case, but for the most part, we must partner in our working relationships to make things happen. Effective networking is the means to do this.

This is not to say that we should build networks with the sole intent to get ahead in life or in the workforce. In contrast, it is the unintentional and ubiquitous relationships that fuel the fire of partnership; especially those without an ulterior motive.

Think back to the playground when you were eight years old. One of the favorite games was kickball, where the survival of the fittest rang true. Teams were chosen, one person at a time, by two team captains. If you were well known, and even if you were not the athletic type, you were typically chosen earlier than the new guy or girl. You may not have realized this at the time, but this was your first exposure to team selection. You were happy when you were ultimately chosen, and respected your Captain for choosing you. You swore allegiance to not let your Captain or your teammates down.

Yet current day team building at school or work cannot be comparable to choosing a kickball team. Or can it?

Are we currently reliving the scenario that we experienced on the playground when we choose current-day team partners, hoping they can deliver the needed home run kick when the bases are loaded?

Ironically, this is exactly what we are doing on a daily basis in our working relationships. We choose partners based upon whom we know, just as a CEO recruits a team, one by one, from her last place of employment. Players capable of hitting the home run, when the bases are loaded; a kickball dream team, of sorts.

Back to the need to develop your network: Most of us are not CEO's with a bench full of team players that we can call on. So how do we start, considering we only know a few good outfielders?

Simple. Do not approach networking with the sole intent of building a dream team. The dream team will come with time. Instead, and as discussed in Chapter 2, assume equality in everyone you meet. Smile when you pass people in the hallway and try to remember their names and call them by name when you see them again. Make a conscious effort to meet a least one new person each week. Over time, you will remember their names, you will remember their faces, and you will grow your network, one person at a time.

There will soon be a day that your network will flourish. The acquaintances that you made will become familiar, and you will become familiar to them. Your network will soon be comprised of great pitchers, excellent fielders, and supportive spectators, willing and ready to be called from the bench.

So, always keep growing by meeting new people, as you build your dream team network.

REFLECTION / PARTING THOUGHTS

PLAY NICE, AND BRING A BALL

How many times does a kickball bring peace to a group of boys on the playground?

Why is it that the girl with the volleyball is everyone's friend?

Consider the premise: We bring, we share, we gain rapport. The ball is irrelevant, as it is just the connection medium. It could instead be a jump rope, a Frisbee, or a favorite book or photo album.

It is possible that there will initially be competition to get the prized ball, but ultimately, the ball becomes the tool to solidify the relationship, by gaining trust.

So, what is the equivalent ball in our current day working relationships? It can be any of the above lessons, whether it be patience, a smile, words of encouragement or a positive compliment. It can be anything that grows your trust and network with your peers. The bottom line is that you must member to bring the ball.

So how can you remember to bring the ball? Simple. Intentionally concentrate on one of the ten working relationship tools each day. Maybe assign two for each work day, and stress these already learned practices from your playground repertoire. Make this a conscious effort, in all of your relationships and daily projects.

They say that practice makes perfect. This, along with the Golden Rule, is incorrect. Practice actually makes "permanent," and not necessarily the learned outcome or behavior that you want.

So concentrate on the outcomes that you desire; be self-aware of how you are treating others on your current day playground; and make "perfect practice" of these 10 tools.

To summarize: Remember to bring the ball or jump rope to the playground. Allow Judy to run to third base without repose. Be patient, and open-minded to different opinions of your study group members. Smile at the people you see every day.

Reclaim and consciously refresh your playground relationship mentality, and build your network and partnerships of the present.

ABOUT THE AUTHOR

David R. Smat is a registered Professional Environmental Engineer in Georgia and Louisiana, with over 28 years of partnership building experience gleaned during his engineering roles in the pharmaceutical, pulp/paper and aerospace industries.

Originally a Chicago native, David currently resides in Fort Worth, Texas, with his wife and four sons, who provide endless relationship building experiences to draw from.

David is in the midst of writing his first novel, named *Double-Take*, planned for publication in late 2015.

44495326R00030

Made in the USA
Lexington, KY
01 September 2015